STEP·BY·STEP
ITALIAN
Cooking

Wendy Berecry

Popular dishes from Italy fully explained and illustrated in easy step-by-step instructions

MURDOCH BOOKS
Sydney • London • Vancouver

Italian family meals generally start with a simple antipasto. This can be a selection of salami, seafoods, olives, cheeses, and piquant bottled vegetables or simply fresh vegetables, dressed with good olive oil.

Seafood Tomato Soup

Use only fresh herbs.

Preparation time: 20 minutes
Cooking time: 15 minutes
Serves 4

750 g mussels in shell
500 g boneless fish fillets
750 g green prawns
250 g small squid tubes
2 tablespoons olive oil
1 onion, chopped
1 cup sliced fennel
2 cloves garlic, crushed
2 small red chillies, finely chopped
1 x 425 g can tomatoes
2 tablespoons tomato paste
2 L fish stock
1/4 cup chopped parsley

1 Add mussels to a pan of simmering water and remove from heat when shells open. Remove mussels from shells, discarding any that do not open. Reserve four shells for garnish and discard the rest.

2 Cut fish fillets into bite-sized pieces. Peel and devein prawns and slice squid tubes into rings.

3 Heat oil in a large pan. Add onion, fennel, garlic and chilli; cook until tender.

4 Add undrained, crushed tomatoes, tomato paste, fish stock and parsley; bring to boil. Reduce heat to low, cover and simmer for 5 minutes.

5 Add seafood; simmer gently for 3 minutes or until seafood is just cooked.

Use scissors to remove cooked mussels from shells.

Cube fish, peel and devein prawns, and slice squid into rings.

Add finely chopped parsley to soup. Simmer for 5 minutes.

Add prepared seafood and simmer gently for 3 minutes.

Meatball, Bean and Macaroni Soup

Preparation time:
20 minutes
Cooking time:
30 minutes
Serves 6

500 g minced steak
1 cup fresh breadcrumbs
1/3 cup tomato paste
2 teaspoons dried oregano leaves
oil for shallow frying
2 L chicken stock
2 onions, chopped
2 potatoes, diced
2 carrots, diced
1/2 cup small macaroni
1 cup shelled peas
1 x 310 g can red kidney beans, drained

1 Combine mince, breadcrumbs, tomato paste and oregano. Roll heaped teaspoonfuls of mixture into balls.

2 Heat oil in frying pan. Add meatballs and fry gently on all sides until golden brown and cooked. Drain on paper.

3 Combine stock, onion, potato and carrot in pan and bring to boil. Add macaroni, cover and simmer for 10 minutes or until vegetables and macaroni are tender.

4 Add meatballs, peas and kidney beans. Simmer 5 minutes.

Knead mince, breadcrumbs, tomato paste and oregano until smooth.

Drain cooked meatballs on absorbent paper.

Add macaroni to soup mixture and cook until just tender.

Stir in meatballs, peas and kidney beans. Simmer 5 minutes.

Golden Fried Garfish with Sambuca

8 small garfish
plain flour for dusting
2 eggs
2 tablespoons chopped parsley
2 tablespoons grated Parmesan cheese
2 tablespoons sambuca
freshly ground black pepper
60 g butter
lemon wedges

Preparation time: 10 minutes
Cooking time: 3 minutes
Serves 4

1 Cut heads from garfish. Cut along underside of fish, open out and press flat. With skin side up, press along backbone, then pull backbone away. Wash and drain.

2 Dust garfish lightly with flour. Combine lightly beaten eggs, parsley, Parmesan cheese, sambuca and pepper; add fish and toss to coat.

3 Melt butter in a frying pan and add garfish in a single layer. Fry on both sides for 1 minute or until lightly browned and cooked through. Drain on absorbent paper and serve with lemon wedges and parsley.

HINT
Fresh sardines can be used instead of garfish. They are stronger in flavour and most plentiful in winter.

Cut heads from garfish, open out and press flat.

Use a small sharp knife to ease away backbone.

Coat flour-dusted fish with egg mixture.

Pan-fry garfish a few at a time until lightly golden.

Mixed Antipasto Platter

Preparation time: 45 minutes
Cooking time: 30 minutes
Serves 4

Frittata Wedges
4 eggs
2/3 cup cream
2 tablespoons grated Parmesan cheese
6 slices Italian salami, finely chopped
1 tablespoon chopped basil

Grilled Mussels
500 g mussels in shell
2 tablespoons lemon juice
1 clove garlic, crushed
1 small red chilli, finely chopped

1 To make the Frittata Wedges, whisk eggs and cream until combined; stir in cheese, salami and basil.
2 Spoon mixture into greased 20 cm pie plate and bake in moderate oven (180°C) for 25 minutes or until set and golden brown. Cool to room temperature; cut into small wedges to serve.
3 For Grilled Mussels, place mussels in pan of simmering water. Remove mussels as shells open; discard any that do not open.
4 Open out mussels and loosen from shells using scissors. Return mussels to half shells; discard other shells.
5 Combine lemon juice, garlic and chilli; spoon over mussels. Place on grill tray and grill on medium until heated through. Sprinkle mussels with parsley to serve.
6 To complete Antipasto Platter, place Frittata Wedges and Grilled Mussels on a large platter and add olives, bottled artichoke hearts and slices of tomato and mozzarella or bocconcini cheese. Arrange food to make an attractive blend of colours and textures.

Combine grated cheese and salami with eggs and cream; mix well.

Spoon mixture into a greased 20 cm pie plate.

Spoon combined lemon juice, garlic and chilli over mussels.

Place mussels on grill tray. Grill until just heated through.

Herb-Marinated Capsicums

4 red capsicums
½ cup olive oil
2 tablespoons lemon juice
1 tablespoon chopped basil
1 tablespoon chopped parsley
2 teaspoons chopped oregano
8 arugula leaves
8 cos lettuce leaves
200 g feta cheese, cubed

Preparation time:
20 minutes + 2 hours marinating
Cooking time:
5 minutes
Serves 4

1 Cut capsicums into quarters; remove stems and seeds. Place skin side up under a preheated grill; cook until skin blisters and turns black. Stand, covered with a clean damp tea-towel, for 5 minutes. Peel away skin and cut each piece into strips.

2 Combine oil, lemon juice, basil, parsley and oregano and add capsicum strips. Marinate for at least 2 hours, or preferably overnight.

3 Serve capsicum strips with arugula and cos lettuce leaves and cheese.

This dish can be served as an entrée or with any meat dish.

Cut capsicums into quarters. Remove stems and seeds.

Carefully peel away blistered skin from capsicums.

Cut the capsicums into long strips, each 2 cm wide.

Pour combined remaining ingredients over capsicums and marinate.

S
P

Carpaccio

400 g beef eye fillet in one piece
olive oil
small block fresh Parmesan cheese
freshly ground black pepper
salt (optional)
lemon wedges

1 Place beef in the freezer for about 2 hours or until firm but not frozen solid. Using a sharp knife, trim away any fat. Slice fillet into wafer thin slices. Lay slices in single layer over serving plates.
2 Drizzle beef with oil. Using a vegetable peeler, shave shreds of Parmesan cheese from the block; sprinkle over beef.
3 Sprinkle with pepper and salt and squeeze lemon juice over meat.

Preparation time: 20 minutes
Cooking time: nil
Serves 4

Choose high quality beef with low fat and sinew for this recipe. The quantities of topping ingredients will vary according to personal taste. Toppings may be served separately for guests to serve themselves.

HINT
Ask your local delicatessen to slice beef with their slicing machine.

Trim fillet of any fat. Slice fillet into wafer-thin slices.

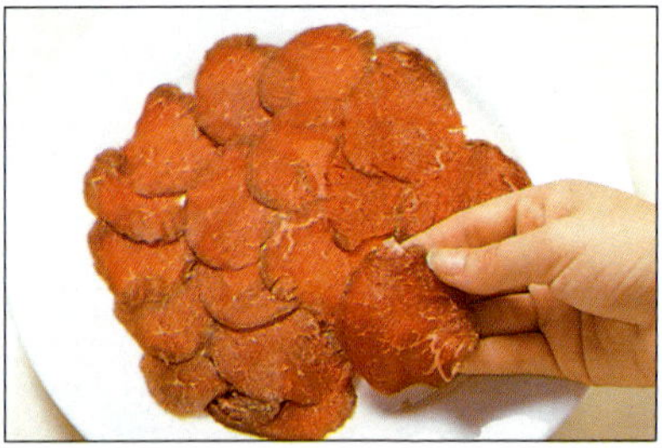

Lay slices in a single layer over serving plate.

Drizzle a good quality olive oil evenly over fillet.

Use a vegetable peeler to shave thin slices of Parmesan.

VEGETABLES AND SALADS

Vegetables play a major role in Italian cuisine. They are served as antipasto, with pasta and as side dishes, the most commonly used being eggplant, capsicum, and zucchini.

Genoese Bean and Potato Bake

"Old" potatoes give the best results.

500 g potatoes
500 g green beans
2 eggs
1/2 cup grated Parmesan cheese
2 tablespoons chopped Italian parsley
2 tablespoons chopped dill
freshly ground black pepper
1 cup fresh breadcrumbs
2 tablespoons olive oil

Preparation time: 20 minutes
Cooking time: 30 minutes
Serves 6

1 Peel and roughly chop potatoes. Cook in boiling water until tender; drain and mash.
2 Meanwhile top and tail beans, chop roughly and cook in boiling water until tender; drain. Mash, blend or process until roughly mashed.
3 Combine potatoes and beans with lightly beaten eggs, Parmesan cheese, parsley, dill and pepper.
4 Spoon into 6 x 1 cup ramekin dishes or spread into a 23 cm pie plate or 1 L dish. Sprinkle with combined breadcrumbs and oil. Bake in moderate oven (180°C) for 30 minutes or until heated through and lightly browned.

This dish may be served with any meat dish or on its own as a light entrée.

HINT
Do not use a food processor or blender to mash potatoes as they may become gluey.

Mash potatoes without milk or butter until smooth.

Process cooked beans until roughly mashed.

Combine potatoes and beans, add Parmesan and mix well.

To make fresh breadcrumbs, remove crusts and process.

Cos Lettuce Salad with Cheese and Walnuts

Preparation time: 15 minutes
Cooking time: 10 minutes
Serves 4

2 slices white or brown bread
30 g butter
2 rashers bacon, chopped
1/2 large cos lettuce
60 g Gorgonzola cheese, crumbled
1/3 cup roughly chopped walnuts

Dressing
1 small egg
1/3 cup olive oil
1 tablespoon lemon juice
2 canned anchovy fillets
1 teaspoon prepared mustard

1 Remove crusts from bread; cut bread into 1 cm cubes. Melt butter in frying pan. Cook bread cubes until brown; drain on absorbent paper.
2 Add bacon to pan. Cook, stirring, until brown; drain on absorbent paper.
3 Break lettuce into bite-sized pieces. Combine in serving bowl with bread cubes, bacon, cheese and walnuts; toss well.
4 To make dressing, gently lower egg into simmering water; cook for 1 minute and remove. Break egg into a blender or processor. Add oil, lemon juice, anchovies and mustard; blend until smooth. Pour over salad just before serving.

HINTS
☐ Bread cubes and bacon are best cooked just before serving, but they can be cooked ahead of time and made crisp again in a moderate oven (180°C) for 5 minutes.
☐ The best type of oil for salad dressings is extra virgin olive oil, made from the first pressing of the olives. Greenish in colour, it is thicker and has a richer flavour and aroma than other olive oils, which are quite satisfactory for cooking.

Cook bread cubes in butter until lightly golden.

Cook bacon, stirring, until it is crisp and brown.

Wash and dry lettuce and break it into bite-sized pieces.

Combine lettuce with bread, bacon, cheese and walnuts.

Cauliflower Neapolitan

1/2 medium-sized cauliflower
1 x 425 g can tomatoes
1 tablespoon olive oil
1 onion, finely chopped
12 stuffed olives, sliced
2 teaspoons chopped capers
1/2 teaspoon sugar

Preparation time: 15 minutes
Cooking time: 10 minutes
Serves 4

1 Cut cauliflower into large florets. Boil, steam or microwave until tender; drain and rinse under cold water.
2 Blend or process undrained, crushed tomatoes until smooth; strain to remove seeds.
3 Heat oil in a frying pan; add onion and cook until tender. Add puréed tomato, olives, capers and sugar; simmer until heated through.
4 Toss cauliflower through sauce and serve immediately.

This dish can be served with any meat course or as part of an antipasto platter. It is useful for entertaining as it can be cooked a day ahead and reheated just before serving.

Wash cauliflower and cut it into large florets.

Strain processed tomatoes through a fine sieve to remove seeds.

Add sliced olives and chopped capers to tomato sauce.

Add cooked cauliflower to sauce. Serve immediately.

Ratatouille with Baked Polenta

Serve with meat dishes.

Preparation time: 30 minutes
Cooking time: 30 minutes
Serves 4

Baked Polenta
3/4 cup self raising flour
1/2 cup polenta
1/4 cup grated Cheddar cheese
2/3 cup milk
60 g butter, melted
1 egg, lightly beaten

Ratatouille
1 large eggplant
4 zucchini
2 tablespoons olive oil
1 onion, sliced
2 cloves garlic, crushed
3 large ripe tomatoes, peeled and chopped
1 green capsicum, sliced
1/4 cup tomato paste
2/3 cup water
1 teaspoon dried oregano leaves
2 teaspoons sugar

1 To make Baked Polenta, combine flour, polenta and cheese in a bowl; make a well in the centre.
2 Combine milk, butter and egg; add to flour mixture and stir until combined.
3 Spoon mixture into a greased 20 cm plate; bake in moderate oven (180°C) for 25 minutes or until cooked and lightly browned.
4 To make Ratatouille, cut eggplant into 2 cm thick slices; cut slices into straws 2 cm wide. Cut zucchini into straws of the same size.
5 Heat oil in a large pan; add onion and garlic and cook until onion is tender.
6 Add eggplant, zucchini, tomato, capsicum, tomato paste, water, oregano and sugar; bring to boil. Reduce heat to low, cover and simmer for 15 minutes or until vegetables are tender. Serve Ratatouille with wedges of hot Baked Polenta.

Add combined milk, butter and egg to flour mixture.

Spoon the mixture into a well greased 20 cm pie plate.

Cut eggplant and zucchini into long strips about 2 cm wide.

Combine all vegetables in a large pan. Add tomato paste.

PASTA, RICE AND PIZZA

To many people Italian cooking means pasta. Here we give you dishes using home-made pasta and pasta asciutta *(dry pasta). Pasta can be served simply with a little butter and cheese or with a rich sauce.*

Spaghetti Puttanesca

Preparation time: 15 minutes
Cooking time: 15 minutes
Serves 4

- *4 large ripe tomatoes (about 750 g)*
- *1 tablespoon olive oil*
- *2 cloves garlic, crushed*
- *2 small red chillies, chopped*
- *1/2 cup water*
- *12 green or black pitted olives, sliced*
- *8 anchovy fillets, chopped*
- *2 teaspoons chopped capers*
- *2 tablespoons chopped parsley*
- *1 tablespoon chopped basil*
- *300 g spaghetti*
- *Parmesan cheese (optional)*

1 Peel and seed tomatoes; chop roughly.

2 Heat oil in pan. Add garlic and chilli; cook over medium heat for 1 minute. Add tomatoes and water; cover. Reduce heat to low and simmer for 10 minutes or until tomatoes become soft and pulpy; add a little extra water if sauce sticks to pan.

3 Add olives, anchovies, capers, parsley and basil; simmer for 3 minutes.

4 Meanwhile, cook spaghetti in boiling water until tender and then drain. Add to sauce and toss over heat until combined. Serve Spaghetti Puttanesca sprinkled with freshly grated Parmesan cheese, if desired.

Peel tomatoes and remove seeds with a teaspoon.

Add water to tomato mixture. Cover and simmer 10 minutes.

Add olives, capers, anchovies and herbs to tomato mixture.

Toss cooked spaghetti and sauce mixture to combine.

Spinach, Ham and Mushroom Lasagne

Preparation time: 30 minutes
Cooking time: 40 minutes
Serves 6

16 large spinach leaves
200 g ricotta cheese
1/2 cup grated Cheddar cheese
2 tablespoons olive oil
1 onion, chopped
2 cloves garlic, crushed
200 g leg ham, chopped
300 g mushrooms, finely chopped
1 x 425 g can tomatoes
1 1/2 cups tomato purée
1/4 cup chopped basil
1 x 250 g packet no-cook lasagne sheets
1/3 cup grated Parmesan cheese

1 Roughly chop spinach. Boil, steam or microwave until tender; drain. Combine with ricotta and Cheddar cheeses.

2 Heat oil in a frying pan, add onion and garlic; cook until onion is tender. Add ham and mushrooms, cook 2 minutes. Add undrained, crushed tomatoes and tomato purée; bring to boil. Reduce heat; simmer 5 minutes or until sauce has reduced and thickened. Stir in basil.

3 Place one-fifth of the lasagne sheets over base of a 3 L oven-proof dish; spread with half the spinach mixture. Top with one-fifth lasagne sheets, half the ham mixture and one-fifth lasagne sheets. Repeat layering with remaining ingredients.

4 Sprinkle with Parmesan cheese. Cover dish; bake in moderate oven (180°C) for 30 minutes. Uncover dish; bake further 10 minutes or until lasagne is tender.

HINT
For a vegetarian lasagne, replace ham with 2 x 310 g cans red kidney beans, drained.

Combine spinach, ricotta and Cheddar cheese. Mix well.

Add tomato purée to ham and mushroom mixture.

Spread half the spinach mixture over lasagne sheets.

Top spinach mixture with lasagne and then ham. Repeat layers.

Penne Pasta with Creamy Seafood Sauce

500 g green prawns
300 g white fish fillets
200 g scallops
90 g smoked salmon
2 cups chicken stock
30 g butter
1 onion, chopped
1 clove garlic, crushed
3/4 cup cream
2 tablespoons lemon juice
500 g dried penne pasta
2 egg yolks
1 tablespoon chopped basil

Preparation time: 20 minutes
Cooking time: 20 minutes
Serves 6

1 Peel and devein prawns, cut fish into 3 cm cubes, remove any bones. Clean scallops and cut salmon into strips.

2 Bring stock to boil. Add prawns and simmer 1 minute or until prawns change colour; remove. Add fish and simmer 1 minute or until fish changes colour; remove. Add scallops and simmer 1 minute or until scallops change colour; remove. Set stock and seafood aside.

3 Melt butter in pan, add onion and garlic; cook over medium heat until onion is tender.

4 Add stock, cream and lemon juice; bring to boil. Reduce heat to medium; simmer 5 minutes or until sauce is reduced by half.

5 Meanwhile, cook pasta in boiling water until tender; drain.

6 Add all seafood to sauce, return to simmering point. Remove from heat and quickly stir in beaten egg yolks and basil. Pour over hot pasta to serve.

HINTS

☐ Any seafood is suitable for this sauce — try mussels, oysters or calamari. Any kind of fish fillets can be used — whatever is cheapest and most plentiful. Take advantage of seasonal gluts.

☐ Seafood needs little more than heating through to cook. It becomes dry and tough if overcooked.

Peel and devein prawns, cut fish, clean scallops and slice salmon.

Add stock to cream mixture. Bring to the boil, stirring.

Add all prepared seafood to cream mixture.

Remove from heat and stir in beaten egg yolks and basil.

Pumpkin Ravioli with Browned Butter and Pecorino

Preparation time: 1 hour
Cooking time: 5 minutes
Serves 4

Pumpkin filling
500 g piece pumpkin
1/4 cup chopped chives
pinch ground nutmeg

Ravioli dough
2 1/2 cups plain flour
pinch salt
4 eggs, lightly beaten
1 egg for glazing, lightly beaten

Sauce
125 g unsalted butter
freshly grated pecorino cheese
chives

1 To make filling, place pumpkin in a small baking dish, bake in moderate oven (180°C) for 1 hour or until tender; cool. Remove any seeds, scoop out pumpkin and mash with a fork. Combine pumpkin with chives and nutmeg.

2 To make ravioli dough, sift flour and salt into a bowl. Make a well in the centre and add the 4 beaten eggs; gradually incorporate into flour with a fork. Turn onto a lightly-floured surface and knead lightly until smooth and elastic, about 5 minutes. Cover; stand for 30 minutes.

3 Roll out a quarter of the dough very thinly into a rectangle, using a rolling pin or pasta rolling machine. Roll out another quarter to a rectangle slightly bigger than the first.

4 On the first rectangle place teaspoonfuls of pumpkin filling at 5 cm intervals in straight rows. Brush the dough between the filling very lightly with beaten egg. Place second sheet of dough carefully over top. Press down between the filling to seal the sheets of dough together.

5 Use a floured crimped pastry wheel or a sharp knife to cut into squares. Repeat with remaining dough and filling. Place completed ravioli in single layer on a lightly floured tray until ready to cook; cover tray.

6 To cook ravioli, drop into a large pan of boiling water. Cook until tender, about 4 minutes; drain. Transfer to serving plate and keep warm.

7 Heat butter in a pan over medium heat until lightly browned, but not burnt; pour over ravioli. Sprinkle with pecorino cheese to serve; garnish with extra chives.

Dough and filling can be made the day before. Assemble up to two hours ahead.

Place teaspoonfuls of pumpkin filling at 5 cm intervals.

Brush the dough between filling with lightly beaten egg.

Press second sheet of dough between filling to seal.

Use a floured crimped pastry wheel to cut into squares.

Spinach, Cheese and Pancetta Pasta Shells

Preparation time: 30 minutes
Cooking time: 10 minutes
Serves 4

16 giant pasta shells
1 tablespoon olive oil
1 onion, chopped
125 g pancetta, chopped
2 cloves garlic, crushed
12 large spinach leaves
2 ripe tomatoes, peeled, chopped
250 g ricotta cheese
2 tablespoons chopped basil
ground nutmeg, to taste
½ cup grated Parmesan cheese

Tomato sauce
1 x 425 g can tomatoes
1 tablespoon tomato paste
1 teaspoon sugar

1 Cook pasta shells in boiling water until just tender. Drain, rinse under cold water and drain again.
2 Combine oil, onion, pancetta and garlic in frying pan. Cook over medium heat until onion is tender.
3 Remove spinach stalks and chop leaves finely. Add spinach and tomato to pan; cook until tender.
4 Remove from heat. Stir in ricotta cheese, basil and nutmeg. Spoon into pasta shells, place on a greased baking tray and sprinkle with Parmesan cheese. Bake in moderate oven (180°C) for 10 minutes or until heated through. Serve with Tomato Sauce.
5 To prepare Tomato Sauce, blend or process undrained tomatoes until smooth; strain to remove seeds. Combine in small pan with tomato paste and sugar. Bring to boil; reduce heat and simmer 3 minutes.

HINT
Cook pasta shells until just tender. Overcooking will result in shells tearing.

Cook onion, garlic and pancetta until onion is soft.

Add the chopped peeled tomatoes to spinach mixture.

Stir in ricotta, basil and nutmeg to spinach mixture.

Use a teaspoon to carefully fill pasta shells.

Porcini Mushroom and Onion Risotto

1 x 15 g packet sliced dried porcini mushrooms
1 L chicken stock
60 g butter
2 onions, chopped
1 clove garlic, crushed
1 1/2 cups arborio rice
150 g fresh mushrooms, chopped
2 tablespoons chopped parsley
1/4 cup grated Parmesan cheese

1 Soak porcini mushrooms in cup hot water for 45 minutes; drain. Bring chicken stock to boil.

Preparation time: 10 minutes + 45 minutes soaking
Cooking time: 30 minutes
Serves 4

2 Meanwhile, melt butter in pan; add onion and garlic and cook over low heat until tender and brown.
3 Add rice; stir until combined. Add 1 cup simmering stock and bring to boil. Cook until liquid has almost evaporated, stirring often.
4 Add another 1 cup stock; cook until liquid has almost evaporated, stirring often. Add porcini and fresh mushrooms and continue adding stock as above. It should take about 20 minutes from the first addition to add all the stock.
5 Reduce heat to low; stir in parsley and Parmesan cheese. Cover; cook 2 minutes and serve immediately.

Adding stock gradually to the rice is the traditional way to cook risotto to give a creamy texture. It should be served immediately.

HINT
Porcini mushrooms are wild mushrooms which impart a very strong flavour. They are available at delicatessens only in dried form. If unavailable, substitute with an extra 200 g of fresh mushrooms.

Add arborio rice to onion and butter mixture.

Pour 1 cup chicken stock over rice and cook until evaporated.

Add porcini mushrooms and fresh mushrooms to rice mixture.

Stir in parsley and Parmesan cheese; cook 2 minutes.

Traditional Crispy Pizza

Preparation time:
30 minutes
Cooking time:
30 minutes
Serves 4

Crust
7 g dried yeast
2 teaspoons sugar
3/4 cup warm water
2 1/2 cups plain flour
pinch salt

Topping
3/4 cup bottled tomato pasta sauce
125 g Italian salami, sliced and cut into strips
2 tablespoons chopped basil
125 g small cap mushrooms, sliced
1 onion, sliced into thin wedges
1/2 green capsicum, sliced
12 pitted black olives, halved
6 anchovy fillets
1 cup grated mozzarella cheese
1/4 cup grated Parmesan cheese

1 To prepare crust, combine yeast and sugar in a bowl; stir in warm water.
2 Sift flour and salt into a bowl; add yeast mixture and stir until combined.
3 Knead dough on lightly floured surface for 10 minutes or until smooth and elastic. Roll out to a circle large enough to fit a 30 cm pizza tray.
4 Spread pizza with tomato sauce and top with salami, basil, mushrooms, onion, capsicum and olives. Lay anchovies over top; sprinkle with mozzarella and Parmesan cheeses.
5 Bake in moderately hot oven (190°C) for 30 minutes.

HINT
For a pizza with a difference, divide dough in half. Roll one piece into a 25 cm circle and pile half the topping ingredients onto one side of it. Fold dough over to form a semicircle; press edges together. Repeat with remaining dough and topping. Place on a baking tray; bake at 190°C for 30 minutes.

Add yeast, sugar and water mixture to sifted flour.

Use a rolling pin to roll dough out to a 30 cm round.

Spread bottled tomato sauce evenly over pizza base.

Scatter pizza evenly with toppings. Lay anchovies on top.

MEAT AND CHICKEN

Italy is famous for its veal dishes. In this chapter we give you quick and easy recipes for Veal Scaloppine and Veal with Sage and Lemon. Braised chicken with wine, herbs and garlic also features.

Beef and Bocconcini Salad with Pesto Dressing

Preparation time: 25 minutes
Cooking time: 20 minutes
Serves 4

500 g piece eye fillet beef
freshly ground black pepper
1 tablespoon olive oil
30 g butter
6 bocconcini
8 bottled or canned artichoke hearts, drained
4 bottled or canned pimientos, drained
8 radicchio lettuce leaves

Pesto Dressing
1/2 cup olive oil
1 tablespoon lemon juice
1/4 cup firmly packed Italian parsley
1/4 cup firmly packed basil leaves
1 tablespoon capers

1 Tie beef with string to help hold its shape during cooking; sprinkle liberally with pepper. Heat oil and butter in a baking dish; add beef and fry on all sides until brown. Transfer to moderately hot oven (190°C); cook for 20 minutes, or longer if you prefer beef medium or well done. Allow to cool at room temperature before slicing.
2 Slice bocconcini, halve artichoke hearts and cut pimientos into strips. Arrange on serving plate with lettuce and beef slices.
3 To prepare dressing, combine oil, lemon juice, parsley, basil and capers in a blender or food processor; blend until smooth.

Place beef in baking tray and fry on all sides till brown.

Halve artichoke hearts and thinly slice bocconcini.

Cut the drained pimientos into long thin strips.

Combine oil, lemon juice, basil, parsley and capers.

Veal Scaloppine with Eggplant and Tomato

Preparation time: 25 minutes
Cooking time: 20 minutes
Serves 4

4 large pieces veal scaloppine
plain flour for dusting
60 g butter
1 small eggplant, thinly sliced
1 large tomato, thinly sliced
4 slices fontina cheese
2 teaspoons dried oregano leaves
freshly ground black pepper

1 Dust veal with flour. Heat butter in a frying pan until beginning to brown. Add veal in single layer. Brown quickly on both sides, about 30 seconds; remove.

2 Add eggplant slices to pan. Fry on both sides until brown; remove.

3 Lay each veal slice on a large sheet of foil; top with eggplant, tomato then cheese. Sprinkle with oregano and pepper.

4 Bring foil loosely up around veal to make a package; seal at the top, leaving space between the foil and cheese. Place packages on a baking tray; bake in moderate oven (180°C) for 20 minutes or until vegetables are tender.

Dust veal with flour and brown both sides quickly in butter.

Lay veal, eggplant and tomato slices over large sheets of foil.

Place sliced cheese over tomato and sprinkle with oregano.

Bring foil up loosely around veal to form a package.

Veal Chops with Sage and Lemon

Preparation time:
10 minutes
Cooking time:
10 minutes
Serves 4

4 veal loin chops
plain flour for dusting
1 egg, beaten
2 tablespoons milk
3/4 cup dried breadcrumbs
1 tablespoon finely chopped fresh sage or 2 teaspoons dried sage
30 g butter
1 tablespoon olive oil
1 clove garlic, crushed
lemon wedges

1 Trim fat from chops; curl up tail of chops and secure in place with toothpicks.
2 Dust chops with flour. Brush with combined egg and milk and coat in combined breadcrumbs and sage.
3 Heat butter, oil and garlic in a large fry pan. Add chops in single layer; fry on both sides over medium heat until cooked through. Serve with lemon wedges.

HINT
To make your own dried breadcrumbs, place slices of stale bread and crusts on a baking tray; bake in a slow oven (150°C) until golden brown, dry and crisp. Use a rolling pin or food processor to crush bread into crumbs.

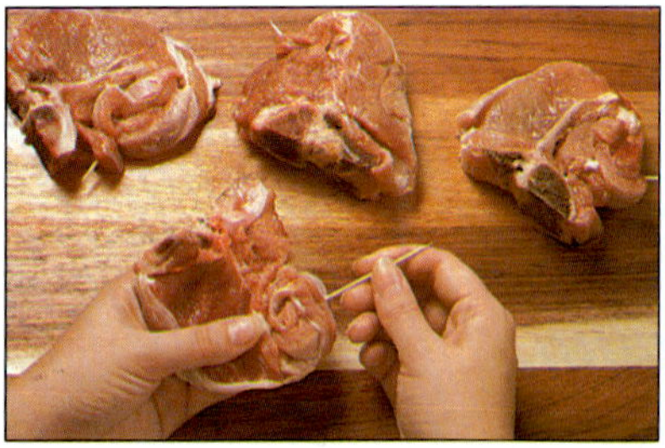

Curl up tails of veal chops and secure with toothpicks.

Brush each chop well with combined egg and milk.

Coat each veal chop evenly with breadcrumb mixture.

Add chops to pan in a single layer. Cook on a medium heat.

Prosciutto Chicken with Anchovy Butter

Preparation time: 30 minutes
Cooking time: 20 minutes
Serves 4

8 small chicken breast fillets
1/3 cup chopped parsley
1/4 cup grated Parmesan cheese
2 teaspoons grated lemon rind
2 cloves garlic, crushed
2 tablespoons sour cream
4 slices prosciutto
1/2 cup white wine

Anchovy Butter
4 egg yolks
4 canned anchovy fillets
2 teaspoons prepared mustard
2 tablespoons lemon juice
125 g butter, melted

1 Pound fillets to flatten them slightly; place cut side up on work surface.
2 Combine parsley, Parmesan cheese, lemon rind, garlic and sour cream. Spread over half of each chicken fillet. Cut prosciutto slices crossways in half; lay a piece over each fillet.
3 Fold fillets in half to enclose filling; secure with toothpicks. Place in a baking dish in single layer; pour in wine. Cover and bake in moderate oven (180°C) for 20 minutes or until chicken is just cooked; drain.
4 To make Anchovy Butter, combine egg yolks, anchovy fillets, mustard and lemon juice in a blender or food processor; blend until smooth. With motor running, pour in hot, bubbly melted butter. Pour over chicken and serve immediately.

HINT
Anchovy Butter can be prepared up to 8 hours ahead to point of adding butter. Add melted butter just before serving.

Spread chicken fillets with sour cream and cheese mixture.

Place prosciutto slices over chicken, fold and secure.

Place chicken in baking dish and pour in the wine.

Pour hot, bubbly, melted butter into processor.

Braised Chicken in Lemon, Garlic and Rosemary

Preparation time: 20 minutes
Cooking time: 40 minutes
Serves 4

1 x 1.5 kg chicken
2 tablespoons olive oil
30 g butter
4 cloves garlic, crushed
1 tablespoon rosemary leaves
2 small red chillies, chopped
1/2 cup white wine
strips of peel from half a lemon
1/4 cup lemon juice
1/2 cup chicken stock

1 Cut chicken into serving-sized portions.
2 Heat oil and butter in a large frying pan. Add chicken pieces in single layer; cook over medium heat until browned. Turn chicken occasionally to prevent sticking.
3 Add garlic, rosemary, chilli and wine. Cover pan, reduce heat to low and simmer for 40 minutes or until chicken is tender.
4 Remove chicken and keep warm. Scoop excess fat from the surface of the pan juices. Add lemon peel, lemon juice and stock. Bring to boil; cook 3 minutes. Pour over chicken pieces to serve.

Brown chicken in butter and oil. Turn to prevent sticking.

Pour wine over chicken, chilli and rosemary.

Remove cooked chicken from pan using a slotted spoon.

Add stock to pan with lemon juice and peel. Simmer 3 minutes.

Olive and Pimiento-Stuffed Chicken Fillets

Preparation time: 15 minutes
Cooking time: 15 minutes
Serves 4

8 chicken thigh fillets
half a 425 g can pimientos, drained
12 pitted black olives
12 pitted green olives
1 small red chilli, halved and seeded
1 clove garlic
6 large basil leaves
1 tablespoon oil
30 g butter
1 cup water or white wine

1 Lay chicken, cut side up, on work surface. Use a meat mallet to flatten fillets slightly.
2 Cut pimientos into pieces large enough to cover one half of each fillet.
3 Combine black and green olives, chilli, garlic and basil in a food processor or blender. Blend until finely chopped (this can be done by hand); spoon onto pimiento.
4 Fold fillet in half to enclose filling; secure with toothpicks.
5 Heat oil and butter over low heat in a large frying pan; add chicken in single layer. Increase heat to medium and fry chicken on both sides until brown. Use a spatula to loosen chicken from base of pan occasionally to prevent sticking.
6 Add water or wine to pan; cover. Bring to the boil, reduce heat to low and simmer for 10 minutes or until chicken is cooked. Serve chicken with pan juices.

HINTS

☐ Pimiento (Spanish for capsicum) is cooked and peeled before being canned or bottled. It is delicious in salads and casseroles.
☐ Use leftover chicken meat and bones (or buy a bag of chicken bones) to make your own chicken stock. Place meat and bones in a pan with a few vegetables — onion, carrot and celery — and flavourings. Cover with water and simmer for 2 hours.

Place chicken between two sheets of plastic wrap and flatten.

Finely chop olives, chilli, garlic and basil or process them in a blender.

Spoon olive mixture evenly over pimiento, fold and secure.

Pour water over chicken in pan, cover and reduce heat.

SEAFOOD

Almost completely surrounded by sea, Italy enjoys much varied seafood. Fresh fish is enhanced with lemon, olive oil and aged vinegars.

Peppered Prawns with Fennel

Celery can replace fennel.

Preparation time: 25 minutes
Cooking time: 10 minutes
Serves 4

- *1.5 kg green prawns*
- *1 tablespoon olive oil*
- *30 g butter*
- *1 onion, cut into eighths*
- *1 fennel bulb, sliced*
- *1 red capsicum, cut into strips*
- *2 cloves garlic, crushed*
- *3 teaspoons freshly ground black pepper*
- *2 tablespoons brandy*
- *1 tablespoon tomato paste*

1 Peel and devein prawns, leaving tail intact.
2 Heat oil and butter in frying pan. Add onion, fennel and capsicum; cook over medium heat until almost tender.
3 Add garlic, pepper and prawns; cook till prawns change colour.
4 Add brandy and tomato paste and stir over heat 1 minute.

Peel and devein prawns, leaving tail section intact.

Cook onion, fennel and capsicum in a pan until tender.

Add garlic, pepper and prawns. Cook, stirring, 3 minutes.

Add tomato paste and brandy to pan. Cook, stirring, 1 minute.

Fried Whitebait with Chilli and Herb Mayonnaise

Preparation time: 30 minutes
Cooking time: 10 minutes
Serves 4

500 g whitebait
plain flour for dusting
1 egg, lightly beaten
3 tablespoons milk
oil for deep frying

Chilli and Herb Mayonnaise
1/2 cup mayonnaise
2 red chillies, finely chopped
2 teaspoons lemon juice
2 teaspoons chopped parsley
2 teaspoons chopped basil
2 teaspoons chopped capers

1 Wash whitebait and dry with absorbent paper. Toss in flour and dip in combined egg and milk.
2 Heat oil in a large pan. Add whitebait in batches and cook for a few minutes until golden brown. Remove and drain on absorbent paper. Keep warm while cooking remaining batches.
3 To make Chilli and Herb Mayonnaise, combine mayonnaise with chillies, lemon juice, parsley, basil and capers. Serve in a bowl as a dipping sauce for whitebait.

Whitebait are tiny, tasty saltwater fish. They are so small that it is not necessary to clean them before cooking and both the head and tail are eaten.

HINTS
☐ To keep herbs fresh, wrap in a damp tea-towel and store in refrigerator.
☐ It is advisable to wear gloves when chopping chillies because they can irritate the skin. If you find it easier you can use scissors instead of a knife. Remember that the seeds are the hottest part so remove them if you want to reduce the heat.

Dip the floured whitebait in combined egg and milk.

Add whitebait in small batches to oil and cook until golden.

Use a large metal strainer to remove whitebait.

Add chillies, juice, parsley, basil and capers to mayonnaise.

Fresh Tuna with Herbs and Balsamic Vinegar

Preparation time:
5 minutes
Cooking time:
10 minutes
Serves 4

4 tuna steaks
2 tablespoons olive oil
1 tablespoon chopped parsley
1 tablespoon chopped basil
2 tablespoons balsamic vinegar

1 Heat oil in a large frying pan. Add tuna steaks in single layer and cook on both sides over medium heat for about 10 minutes or until cooked. Time will depend on thickness of tuna steak.

2 Transfer tuna steaks to serving plate. Sprinkle with parsley and basil; drizzle with balsamic vinegar.

HINTS

☐ Fresh tuna becomes dry if overcooked. Ideally it should still be pink in the centre. If tuna is not available, use any fish cutlet or fillet. Tuna steaks can be grilled instead of fried.

☐ Balsamic vinegar comes from Modena in Italy. It is made from unfermented white wine grapes and aged in the same way as wine, giving a richer flavour. Balsamic vinegar is 20 years old before it is sold. If unavailable, red wine vinegar can be used instead.

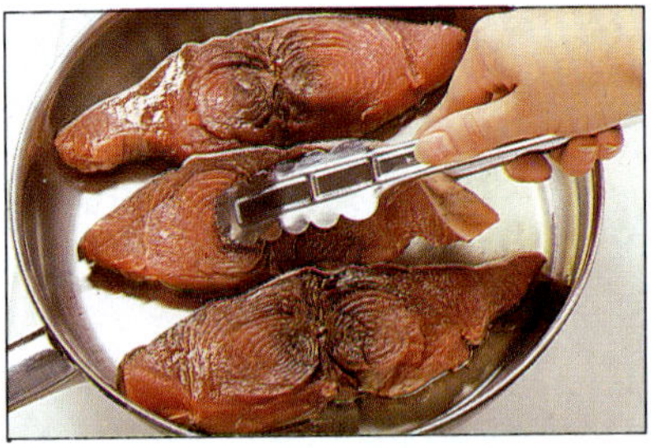

Put the tuna steaks in a large pan in a single layer.

Turn tuna steaks only once to cook both sides.

Place tuna steaks on serving platter. Sprinkle with parsley and basil.

Spoon balsamic vinegar over tuna and serve immediately.

DESSERTS AND CAKE

Desserts are sweet and lush or simply elegant in the Italian cuisine. Traditional favourites can be found in this mouth-watering chapter.

Lemon Zabaglione

Preparation time: 5 minutes
Cooking time: 5 minutes
Serves 4

3 egg yolks
1/4 cup sugar
1 1/2 tablespoons Marsala
1/4 cup lemon juice
1/2 cup white wine
8 almond biscuits

1 Whisk egg yolks and sugar in a heatproof bowl until light and creamy. Add Marsala, lemon juice and wine. Whisk until combined.
2 Place bowl over a pan of simmering water. Stir over heat for 5 minutes or until mixture has thickened.
3 Spoon into serving glasses and serve with biscuits.

HINT
Zabaglione can be served on its own or as a topping for fruit or ice cream. It is quite rich so only small amounts are served.

Whisk egg yolks and sugar in a heatproof bowl until creamy.

Pour in Marsala, lemon juice and wine. Whisk well.

Place bowl over simmering water, stirring until thickened.

Spoon Zabaglione into serving glasses. Serve with biscuits.

Tirami Su

4 egg yolks
1/3 cup caster sugar
1/4 cup milk
250 g mascarpone
3 egg whites
250 g packet savoiardi or sponge fingers
1 1/2 cups cold coffee
1 tablespoon cocoa

Preparation time: 20 minutes
Cooking time: 5 minutes plus 6 hours refrigeration
Serves 6

1 Beat egg yolks and sugar in a heatproof bowl until light and creamy. Add milk and beat until combined.
2 Place bowl over a pan of simmering water. Stir over heat until thickened; allow to cool.
3 Add mascarpone to mixture; stir until combined. Beat egg whites until soft peaks form; fold into mixture.
4 Dip savoiardi biscuits quickly into coffee — they should be moist but not soggy. Place a quarter of the biscuits over base of a 1.5 L serving dish or a paper-lined loaf pan. Spread with one-third of the mascarpone mixture. Repeat layering with remaining biscuits and mascarpone.
5 Cover and refrigerate at least 6 hours, preferably overnight. Sift cocoa over top to serve. If you are using a loaf pan, the Tirami Su can be turned out onto a serving plate, sifted with cocoa and then served sliced.

HINTS

- Espresso or filter coffee has the best flavour for this recipe, but instant coffee can be used.
- Mascarpone is fresh cream to which an acid ingredient, such as lemon juice, has been added. The mixture is then allowed to stand for a few days until it clots. Mascarpone has a creamy texture and a slightly acidic taste, similar to sour cream or crème fraîche. It can be flavoured with a liqueur.

Add mascarpone to egg mixture; stir until combined.

Fold egg whites into egg mixture, using a metal spoon.

Dip savoiardi biscuits quickly into coffee. They should be moist but not soggy.

Repeat layers of mascarpone mixture and savoiardi biscuits.

Lemon Lime Gelato

Preparation time: 25 minutes
Cooking time: 10 minutes plus freezing time
Serves 4

2 cups water
1 cup sugar
$^3/_4$ cup lemon juice
$^3/_4$ cup lime juice
2 egg whites

1 Combine water and sugar in a pan; stir over heat until dissolved. Bring to boil. Reduce heat to low and simmer 10 minutes; cool.
2 Add lemon and lime juice to syrup; pour into large shallow container. Freeze for 1 hour or until mixture is firm but not solid.
3 Turn mixture into a food processor or electric mixer. Add egg whites; blend until smooth. Return to freezer container. Freeze until firm.

HINTS

☐ For a delicious raspberry gelato, blend or process 200 g fresh or thawed frozen raspberries until smooth. Strain to remove seeds. Use only half quantity of citrus juice and add the raspberry purée along with the juice.
☐ Any fresh citrus juices can be used to make this recipe, either alone or in combination, for example orange, mandarin or tangelo, as well as lemon and lime.

Combine water and sugar in pan; stir over heat until dissolved.

Add lemon juice and lime juice to cooled sugar syrup.

Beat frozen mixture with a mixer. Beat in egg whites.

Return mixture to freezing container. Freeze until firm.

Chocolate Ricotta Torte

Preparation time: 30 minutes
Cooking time: 40 minutes
Serves 8

Ideal for a celebration.

Cake
125 g butter, softened
1 cup caster sugar
2 eggs
1 1/4 cups self-raising flour
1/2 cup cocoa
3/4 cup water

Filling
200 g ricotta cheese
2 tablespoons caster sugar
30 g mixed peel, finely chopped
30 g glacé cherries, finely chopped

Topping
2 teaspoons instant coffee powder
1 teaspoon hot water
300 mL cream

1/4 cup brandy
3/4 cup slivered almonds, toasted

1 To make the cake, combine butter, sugar, eggs, sifted flour and cocoa, and the water in small bowl. Beat with electric mixer for 3 minutes or until mixture is smooth and pale in colour.
2 Pour mixture into a greased and base-lined 23 cm round cake tin. Bake in moderate oven (180°C) for 40 minutes or until cooked; turn onto wire rack to cool. Trim top of cake if necessary to allow cake to sit flat. Cut cake horizontally into 3 layers.
3 To make filling, combine ricotta cheese, sugar, peel and cherries.
4 To make topping, dissolve coffee in water. Whip combined cream and coffee mixture until soft peaks form.
5 To assemble torte, place a layer of cake on serving plate; brush with one third of the brandy and spread with half the ricotta filling. Top with another cake layer; brush with one third of the brandy and spread with remaining ricotta filling. Top with remaining cake layer. Brush with remaining brandy. Spread top and sides of cake with coffee cream. Sprinkle top edge of cake with almonds.

This torte can be made and assembled 2 days ahead. Store, covered, in refrigerator.

HINT
Filled cake (without cream topping) can be frozen for up to one month. Thaw at room temperature before spreading with cream topping.

Trim top of cake if necessary and slice horizontally into 3 layers.

Combine ricotta cheese, sugar, peel and cherries.

Spread ricotta mixture evenly between cake layers.

Spread the top and sides of the cake with coffee cream.

Glossary

Anchovies Small saltwater fish. Can occasionally be bought fresh though usually available in cans or jars. Their flavour is strong. For a milder flavour soak in milk for about 20 minutes before using.

Arborio Rice Large-grained white rice, capable of absorbing a large amount of liquid and so ideal for making risotto.

Arugula Also known as rocket lettuce, arugula is used in salads or sautéed. It has small elongated leaves and a peppery flavour.

Balsamic Vinegar Originally from Modena, Italy, it is aged in the same way as wine, giving a richer flavour.

Bocconcini (see Cheeses)

Capers Flower buds of the caper bush, capers are usually pickled in vinegar. They have a piquant flavour.

Cheeses

Bocconcini Fresh mozzarella cheese, moulded into small patties. Ideal for antipasto and salads.

Feta Crumbly cheese with a robust flavour. Made from sheep's, goat's or cow's milk and stored in brine.

Fontina Soft buttery cheese from Val d'Aosta, northern Italy. Ideal for melting.

Gorgonzola Creamy blue-vein cheese with a pungent flavour, originally from Lombardy.

Mozzarella Smooth, soft, elastic cheese with a mild flavour, ideal for melting.

Parmesan Hard cheese bought in blocks or wedges. For best flavour, store in refrigerator but return to room temperature before serving. Grate only as you need it.

Pecorino Similar to Parmesan cheese, made from sheep's or cow's milk, with a rich, tangy flavour.

Ricotta Fresh, unripened cheese, made during the manufacture of other cheeses, with a soft, creamy texture and a mild, sweetish flavour.

Herbs, Fresh Fresh herbs will give the best and most authentic flavour to Italian cooking. To keep herbs fresh, wrap them in a clean damp tea-towel and store in refrigerator.

Marsala Sweet, fortified wine, originally made near Marsala, Italy.

Mascarpone Sometimes referred to as a cheese, mascarpone is made by adding an acid ingredient, such as lemon juice, to cream. The mixture is allowed to stand until it clots and the excess liquid is strained off. It has a soft creamy texture and a creamy, slightly acidic flavour, similar to sour cream.

Olives Fruit of the olive tree, either picked green or fully ripened and black.

Olive Oil The preferred

oil for Italian cooking. It comes in 3 grades.
1 Extra Virgin Olive Oil — the best quality, made from the first cold pressing of the olives. Greenish in colour and thick, this oil is used in salads and other dishes where flavour is important. Generally not used for cooking.
2 Virgin Olive Oil — made from the second cold pressing of the olives. Gold in colour and moderately thick, this oil is used for marinades, mayonnaise and general cooking.
3 Olive Oil — made from the third pressing olives with heat being applied to extract the oil. A light oil, pale gold in colour, this is best used for deep frying and general cooking.

Pancetta Pork belly, salted, cured and spiced. It can be eaten as it is or cooked with other ingredients.

Pasta Flour and water dough, sometimes with the addition of eggs, rolled and moulded in a huge variety of shapes. Pasta can be home-made or purchased fresh from pasta shops that make it on the premises. Dried pasta is the most readily available. Quality between brands varies, but as a guide, look for pasta made from durum wheat for the best texture and ease of handling.

Pimiento Spanish word for capsicum or pepper. Pimientos are widely used in Italian cooking. The capsicums are peeled first and then preserved in water or oil. Available in cans or jars.

Polenta Also called coarse cornmeal, polenta is used for making a porridge-like mixture to be served with meals or made into a type of bread to be baked or fried.

Porcini Mushrooms Wild mushrooms, imported in dried form. They have a strong flavour and are used sparingly.

Prosciutto Uncooked, unsmoked leg of pork, cured in salt. Can be eaten as it is or cooked with other ingredients.

Sambuca A colourless liqueur with aniseed flavour, sambuca is traditionally served in liqueur glasses with three coffee beans. It is set aflame for a few seconds to roast the beans and release the flavour.

Savoiardi Biscuits Wide, flat sponge finger biscuits.

Squid Tubes Also known as calamari tubes, these are small squid which have been cleaned and skinned before purchase.

Tomatoes For best flavour use only ripe tomatoes. Tomatoes should be ripened at room temperature, not in the refrigerator. Only refrigerate for a short time if tomatoes need to be served cold.

INDEX